Welcome to the World of Rod McKuen!

You'll recognize the emotions and feelings that Rod McKuen so wonderfully expresses in his poetry. The feelings of warmth and freedom, of soft sensuality, of sadness and loneliness, and of friendship.

Rod McKuen's new poems form a unity of friendship, illustrating a pathway through the game of life that will bring the rewards of fulfillment. His new book is a life-plan in the form of poetry from a visionary of America and our modern times.

"Humility is a good synonym for McKuen. So is honesty. Both of these qualities are pretty rare in a culture made up of me's, and they are qualities that move a whole lot of people to buy McKuen's songs and poems and weep openly at his concerts."—Mary Martin Niepold, *The Philadelphia Enquirer*

A Biplane Book

Looking for a friend

Rod McKuen

PUBLISHED BY POCKET BOOKS NEW YORK

A Biplane Book

Another *Original* publication of **POCKET BOOKS**

POCKET BOOKS, a Simon & Schuster division of
GULF & WESTERN CORPORATION
1230 Avenue of the Americas, New York, N.Y. 10020

The photographs that augment the poetry in this book were taken over a twenty year period; much of it during the authors concert tours or visits to foreign countries. Locations include: Brazil, Great Britain, France, Italy, Hong Kong, South Africa, Botswana, Switzerland, Mexico, the Soviet Union and Australia. In the United States: Sausalito, California; Los Angeles; Topeka, Kansas; Florida; New Orleans; New York and Pittsburgh.

Photography by Cecil Beaton, Hy Fujita, Edward Habib McKuen, Rod McKuen, Jim Marshall, Wayne Massie, Helen Miljakovich and James Randall.

Cover photo by David Nutter.

ISBN: 0-671-82695-6

First Pocket Books printing May, 1980

10 9 8 7 6 5 4 3 2 1

POCKET and colophon are trademarks of Simon & Schuster.

Interior design by Jacques Chazaud

Printed in the U.S.A.

COPYRIGHT NOTICES

BY ROD McKUEN

BOOKS

Prose
Finding My Father
An Outstretched Hand

Poetry
And Autumn Came
Stanyan Street & Other Sorrows
Listen to the Warm
Lonesome Cities
In Someone's Shadow
Caught in the Quiet
Fields of Wonder
And to Each Season
Come to Me in Silence
Moment to Moment
Celebrations of the Heart
Beyond the Boardwalk
The Sea Around Me
Coming Close to the Earth
We touch the Sky
Looking for a Friend

Collected Poems
Twelve Years of Christmas
A Man Alone
With Love . . .
The Carols of Christmas
Seasons in the Sun
Alone
*The Rod McKuen Omnibus
Hand in Hand
*The Works of Rod McKuen
Love's Been Good to Me.

Collected Lyrics
New Ballads
Pastorale
The Songs of Rod McKuen
Grand Tour

* Available only in Great Britain

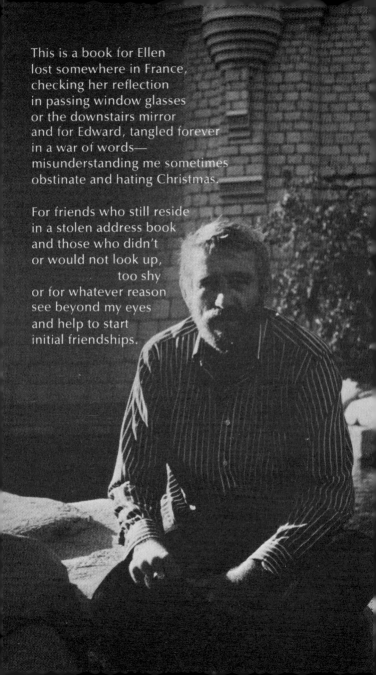

This is a book for Ellen
lost somewhere in France,
checking her reflection
in passing window glasses
or the downstairs mirror
and for Edward, tangled forever
in a war of words—
misunderstanding me sometimes
obstinate and hating Christmas.

For friends who still reside
in a stolen address book
and those who didn't
or would not look up,
                too shy
or for whatever reason
see beyond my eyes
and help to start
initial friendships.

AUTHOR'S NOTE

How far is friendship from love? Not very. Both are immediate needs. Both deserve all the care that we can give them. All the trust that we can muster and let go of, all the selflessness that we too easily forget.

Friendship thrives on love. Love is so much better with friendship added. And life doesn't work very well in the absence of either.

The new poetry collected here—and there is more than usual—is, I think, due in part to the realization that I'm in love or do love very much the close friends I have. Losing even one would leave an emptiness somewhere inside that no amount of rationalization—or even finding someone new—could possibly fill. So while the overriding theme of this book is friendship, it is also a collection of love.

R. M., April 1980

Contents

The Sea, As An Observer

Scaling Walls

Suitcases In Hallways

Some Come As Friends . . . But

Lifted Aloft

Night Mischief

One to One

for MARIAN SELDES

You can widen your life by yourself, but to deepen it you need a friend. Each encounter that becomes a friendship turns into a lifeline. One can never have too many, only too many to properly take care of.

NIGHT WALKER

Go out of an evening
allow yourself the pride
                and punishment
of being jostled by the crowd.
You may begin your preparation
                        early
but do not leave the house
till half past ten or later.

Begin to think about
the night ahead
early in the day.
Make a plan—
not too detailed,
but one that set in motion
will give wheels and
                          turnstiles
to the night as well.

Concentration
during sunlight hours
should offer each of us
              the luxury
of walking through the night
without a stumble
              or a lurch,
missing nothing
catching everything
but allowing us the chance,
the privilege
of being caught.

Streetlights
do not hang like stars
they are strung
like streetlights
but the shadows
they invite and make
are wondrous all the same
hiding places
if you'll hide
finding places
if you're looking—

Go out
of an evening
just to walk.
Smile back,
if smiled at.
Talk, speak up
if you are spoken to.

If the street
is new to you
inquire about
            the shops,
the weather.
Say anything,
but something.

There can be
no initiation
without the firm desire
        of the initiate.

Question
if you're curious
and *listen*
even if the answers
seldom seem
worth hearing.

Remember
that the other walkers
have planned this evening too
and so you have
          a kinship.

Go out alone
and do not be afraid
if you return alone.
Your life has nights
and evenings up ahead
in great abundance.

Even when
you feel you've reached
the end or edge of life,
                    hold on.
Life itself
will ultimately
take care of you.

While loneliness
is part and parcel
of certain days
and certain weeks,
knowing that it is
will help to make you ready
when it comes.

Aloneness
is quite different,
A privilege and a joy
when you've brushed
against too many
                shoulders
in the dim light
        of the disco
or the bright lights
        of the beach.

Don't forget
what you've always known
you are the captain
of your ship
if not the master
of your soul.

Your soul belongs to God,
if your ship goes drifting
He'll guide it back.
Since every walk
however short
is still a voyage
you may chart the trip
even if the destination
                    is unknown.

Avoid all desperation
in the quiet of your room
or at the corner
waiting for the light
                to change.

Desperation is the enemy
of making lasting friends.

Do not be afraid
of fog or cold
approaching mists
or morning coming.

Make way
for children running
down the block.
Leave your watch at home.

Go out of an evening
unmindful of the clock.
Time travels too
and you will learn
with little study
that time becomes a friend
finally and forever—

Do not ask
the definition
of a friend.
He/she is that one
without whose company
death and dying
set in earlier,
         and living
is made more pleasurable.

That is not to say
a friend can make you
                              live,
only that living
for a friend or fancy
is the ultimate,
the road away from self,
the path that leads
from selfishness
to selflessness.

For if you don't know
where you came from
it's hard to ascertain
just where you're going—
in life or down the block.

For now, go out
            of an evening.

You walker
and you walkers
        of the night
I address my words
and worrying to you.

I am involved with you.
Your joys are mine.
Though I have sorrows
        of my own
I'll take on yours,
but in moderation only.
I expect you
to get on with it.
Remember I'm involved
if only silently.
A friend I am
        and will be.

Night walkers
all need friends.

I knew that you
would find me
in the end.

Hello.
Here I am.

I BELIEVE IN ONE TO ONE

To those who've gone past
making my acquaintance
my religion is well known.
I believe in bodies
      arms entangling
          and untangling.
I believe, and I know it to be so
that there are so many curves
          and hollows
in a single body
      that none of us
         not one
can come to know them all
within a lifetime.
Still it's useless
to be alive
and not go right on trying.

My faith is sure.
It cannot be killed
                or stopped
by one opening I wanted
that didn't open
by one mound
that wasn't soft enough
to ease my head,
by one I sought
but didn't win,
by a wound of love
so fresh it hasn't healed.

I believe
in one to one
and one on one.
No wine or magic
no hand-me-down Bible
can improve on that.

I believe in spring
but only if I'm rolling
                    in a pillow
or hold some well-loved face
is any world green enough for me.

ASSESSMENT

In coming back again
in mind and matter
have I learned anything?
        I think not.
The ache is still
as deep as ever,
the hurt will not be muzzled.

I'm stronger though.
Time does that.
Time and thunder.
I pray to God
I'll go on looking
always with a sense of hope
        and wonder.

Looking Backward, Looking Ahead

for ROBERT EGAN

Be on the lookout for the strength in people,
their gentleness and how they smile—on a
given day or through your lifetimes, be on the
lookout. Try to imitate those qualities, making
them *your* perfections. Friendship is fairness.
I have known the most democratic community
to exist of only two people, dedicated to
each other.

LOOKING FOR A FRIEND

If one thousand men
walking through this world
room to room to room
then home again
ask the favor of
      your friendship
know that I am one
within the thousand.

If one hundred men
making do within this world
in city places
or the kindest country
fall down fighting for
      your friendship
know I am on the battlefield
amid the hundred.

If twenty men
who know and knew this world
from crested hills
to uncrowned valley
send letters breathing friendship
expect my letter soon
among the twenty.

If one man
living in this too-grey world
running crooked roads
or pacing pavements
comes in *need* of friendship
be not amazed or disbelieve,
I am that one man.

If no one comes to you
carrying a new world
in his arms or at his back
in a rolling wagon
offering it to you out of friendship
know that I have been detained
but even now am on my way.

Still no one comes
to you within this world
when two dozen years
or half of that has passed
and you feel friendless
come and seek me out
for I'll be lifeless in a grave
                    and gone.

Perhaps you were hiding
or concerned with other
                    larger things
but know that while I lived
I went on looking.

THE DAYS OF THE DANCING, 1965

When I think of love
I think of Line's room
where everything begins and ends,
of songs like *Lilac Wine*
and *When The World Was
        Young*,
of girls I knew
beneath the chinaberry tree
at home when I was younger.

Walking after midnight
                expecting something.
The women in the Silver Dollar Bar
                in San Francisco
rubbing up against the sailors
                        home on leave.
Hearing Beretta sing sad songs
down the alley at The Jackpot.
A girl fanning herself
under a forty-watt bulb
in a room in Teague
offering me and my buddy
                a package job.

Is love collective?
Not anymore it's not.
We're lucky if it lives
above the jukebox bleat.

And so when I think of love
                          and loving
I think of people
dying alone for lack of love.
The skeletons of kites
setting off treetops
and telephone lines.
Wild strawberry blossoms
that decorate hills
of otherwise green.

The solitary things.
For it is not the normal thing
            to love
                    not in these times.
       It goes against the grain.
It is one plane the psychedelic mind
                        has closed.

If not for even breadth
then across the width
and halfway down the length
of this charging decade.

These are the days of the dancing—
                six feet apart.
The discothèque has tapped
        that time of loving into time.

Mr. Roebuck still likes Mr. Sears.
Abercrombie's stuck with Fitch
                all these years.
There must be others out there
                    somewhere.

When I think of love,
　　　　　and I do all the time,
I call up Flo and she says *come on over*
and we'll drive down to Trancas
　　　　　　　　at the beach.
　　　　　　It's something to do.
It is at that.
Better than reading *Alice in Wonderland*
　　　now called *Valley of the Dolls*.

Wonderland is still there waiting, Alice,
it didn't die with Marilyn or Kennedy—
though the Rolling Stones
have killed it once or twice
it's living somewhere in the sticks.

We're only killing off the need.

Remember the athletes' mouths
they used to paint around the hole
                    on Broadway
that puffed out Camel smoke?
                    That was love.
Graffiti on a billboard wall
MAKE DATE—I LUV YOU.
In the end I suppose the athletes
            were not paid enough
to let their mouths be stretched that far.
But oh some tourists
went home happy in those days
                    full of smoky dreams.

The magazines are filled
with foreign bodies now.
They are not love.
We can't identify with them.

When I think of love
I think about the corner bar.
It was always good to me.
But even it's gone topless now.

God let us be different.
Let's not wear mustaches
            and funny clothes.
Let's not let our hair grow so long
it covers up our eyes
and makes us unable to see the world.
Never mind the world—
            let's not miss each other.

They can keep their butterfly collections
their nineteen-thirties songs
            and one-room trips.
I want to see the world
            within the circle of your arms
and sail the wide sea of your thighs.

These are the days of the dancing
                    six feet apart.
And what was your first name anyway?

THE DAYS OF THE DANCING, 1980

I cannot
       imagine
thinking more of love
fifteen years ago
than I do today.

In the cushioned boardroom,
aeroplaning place to place,
walking, riding, flying,
in the X-ray room
or beneath the dentist's drill,
in my living room—
still tongue-tied when friends
bring strangers to my house—

Yes, in rooms and out of rooms
beneath the sky and in it
love dominates all thoughts
and sometimes supercedes
                          true thinking.

The songs are different now.
Those of others and my own.
Titles and a snatch of tune
are for reference only.
And younger days
are sometimes yesterday,
this morning or within the hour.
Beretta's now a mime
in New York City—
lovely as a princess,
though dressed up as a prince.
The lark still lives within her
and if he seldom sings,
when he does, the melody
is more than music, even magic.

There are no Silver Dollar bars
            in San Francisco now
and thus no jackpots to be won.
Hustling is industry,
not done in shadows anymore
and finally if one goes back
no Wasserman need be practiced
                        anymore.
Legions must thank God for that,
            I do.

Loving's even less collective now.
Across the bay the cult of self
has reached proportions laughable
to some, and sad to more.

Still hardly anyone
now dies from lack of love
if his dying place contains
                    a mirror.

The days of the dancing,
                    six feet apart
has now been so refined
that bouncers battle crowds
who come to die in discos.
These deaths are orchestrated
by Rubel, Regine and rhythm-sections
loud enough to make aspirins
                    unnecessary
and elevate the headache
onto a plane above mere pain.

Abercrombie's split with Fitch.
Sears wouldn't speak
to Roebuck if he could.
To send a telegram
down the nearest street
requires a phone call out of state.
Communication? Well, there's public-access
television
and the want-ads too.
But what we want
we do not find
or those of us who do
protect our newfound treasures
as we used to sheath
our duck-tail pocket combs.

When I think of love,
and I do all the time,
I think if I had
        one more lover
I'd be satisfied forever.
Age hasn't made my mind up
but how I've practiced
all these years
I feel I could be good now.
I know I'm finally ready.

I worry too
that in this headlong
        stumble forward
perhaps I missed the great love
or brushed aside
        and didn't pay attention
            to *the moment*—
in my eagerness to investigate
new moments up ahead.

Sometimes it's easy.
Love isn't practiced
            only thought about,
but then the need
like water to the driest land
overtakes me and I'm done.

Just now
want is such a heavy mantle
I'd sign away my eyes
if they'd had a final look
on someone I knew
would be there too
            and waiting
within whatever darkness comes.

These are the days of the dancing
        I now know every step
and I am eager to learn others
        if that will help.

Steve always waves me past the buffalos
and into green grass.
The music's on a roller coaster·
the lights are flashing faster
            than a pulse beat.

It's up to me
to not be carried
too far off by Gloria
and all the glitter.
I too can say *I will survive*.
I must. For even as the years
                    add up
I know that something waits.
There are no boundaries anymore
except one's own good taste.
Pause in the dancing,
stop the speeding light,
try to remember to look around
it always worked before.

And so
it's not the living
            that's important
re-living is the trick.
Remembering is the key
and that one passkey
unlocks all the locks.

I'm here. I'm trying.
Gloria's got it! *I will survive*.
For I have gone
            beyond survival
to another plane
one that demands
a long reach backward
to pull through the rabbit hole
what I passed up
            on the highway
or lost while sparring in the dance.

Happy the days
of the dancing
for they have all
turned into night.

The shadows are softer now
and stars all twinkle
under clapboard skies,
but do not be mistaken
this is reality
as real as any you will find.

I'm moving straight ahead
it's only that I'm finally learning
           to look backward.

I see you.
Well, almost.
You have been
collected in my head
from all the things
I want and wanted
till now, I only await your coming
like the tide
             or some new moon.

I won't forget
your first name this time.
I've practiced free association
till at last I'm free.

Bound by what I need
but free to have it
        if I'll try.

Friendship,
Then Forward

for BERNADETTE PETERS

Don't expect all the world to love you until you've learned to love all the world. It is doubtful you will have the time for such an epic. Friendship? It is only love undeclared, not named. . . as the best and lasting loves are held two-gether by the strength of good friendships.

DISCOVERY

Hold on to me
as no one has
while we settle
soft and simple
amid the city grass.

I ask that you
stay long enough
to help me prove
that I have worth.

You decide.
Am I narrow as the
                    noontide,
am I high enough
to touch a single star?
Will I ever reach
the far field?

Do I have worth enough
to occupy an hour
                    maybe more
within the frame of reference
                    you call time?

Two people living
giving out the best
        to one the other
            a handshake
or a double handstand
taken to its farthest
and most perfect resting place.

The corners of your eyes
but just the corners—
                frown.
What does that mean?

Your nipples now erect
nudge your dress
as if to burrow through.
You haven't smiled
and yet you do.
I wish that I were
            plain enough
to show you I'm but me
or as *fancy* as I feel
you think I should be.

Can you carry me
across the water?
Turn and run
along the sand
with me
our feet not touching even spray
this time.

AND THE HORSE GOES HOME

Rabbits run
geese fly north/south
then homeward, north again.
Every animal or bird
        however small
each thing
that moves beneath
God's benevolent eye
does so only
in God's own good time

Riding in the field
        this morning;
thinking not about
the needs of all men
but selfishly
of my own needs only
I wondered
as I now am wondering
what design
or brand-new plan
God might have in mind
        for me.

When the horse beneath me
begins to stomp and chomp
and gallop through the earth
I often wish that it was
my own muscled flesh
thundering through the field
and up the hillsides
sure of where I headed
or positive
        that whatever hand
that guided me, knew.

Nothing stirs now
no revolution
    has come about
no direction
has changed for me
but I feel
and have been feeling
the need to move.

After the ride,
after all the rides
we head home slowly
   the horse and me.

Not tired but resigned.

SUMMER BEACHES/ WINTER BIRDS

for DIANE BENNETT

All of us, however rich with hours up ahead or
those with hours that even now we're
spending are looking for a friend . . .
and sometimes a friend becomes something more.

PORTRAIT

You run like rivers
not yet sure
of destinations or of roots.
The sweetness of you
covering everything it touches
so that a smell, a feeling
lingers even when you've passed.

Having not yet bitten
or gouged your way
          into the earth
you move directionless
and yet with such a sense
                    of sureness
that almost no one notices
the way that you take over
          everything you touch.
It's as if an alien angel
          arriving in the night
spread her cape
and as it then unfurled
each pass she made
made morning one shade better.

Standing still
you do so in a way
that calm pervades the room,
the garden, hill, the street,
the beach, the world,
where you choose to stand.

You are not so much a woman
                    as you are a wonder
you are not so much
                    a young girl standing
as you are a gift unopened
a flower budding
with weeks away
before your bulge and blossom
                    fill the eye.

Gone a moment,
a day, a month, more,
you are not missed so much
as you are mourned for,
needed, absent as an afternoon
that God forgot to make.

What makes you extra ordinary
                    in every way
is that with you, within my life
no day is ordinary or alike.
While you move easy
                    or stand still,
walk out a room to wherever
know that you have strengthened,
straightened out, set in line,
made my life alive erect forever.

BEHAVIOR AT THE BEACH

I try to keep
from pushing up against you
on the street
     in public places
here at this hardly public beach,
even coming up behind you
softly, stealthily, when we're at home.

Admittedly my effort
to put a hold on how I feel
is hardly any effort at all,
love has taken hold
of any sensibilities I had
        or given me
so many senses of another kind
that even your embarrassment
        at open fondling
that should be saved for privacy
fails to keep my hands
in even well-worn pockets.

Just now
the beach is filled
with people making love
and building several hundred
            unimportant conversations.
We say nothing.
There is no necessity for speech
                    between us
but I roll over every twenty minutes
to rub you down with oil
            supposedly against the sun,
'til finally you're layered
like a channel swimmer
or a lacquer box in progress.
I doubt the sun will find its way
through so much petroleum.

The day done we'll go home
and you'll be paler than an egg.

Did I really once perceive you
                as a friend?
Oh you are, but so much more.
I hope my trusted friends
of long standing and seniority
will understand why I've become
to them a missing person.
If they came upon me now
I'm sure they'd find me certifiable
for any institution they could name.

Come into the water.
With fingers crossed
I promise I'll behave—
besides you're slippery
as an overflowing lamp.
I'll scrub your back
with cool, wet sand.
You can float head up,
face down, at your pleasure
supported by my forearm
steady underneath your breasts.

You see, I can be counted on
to be good natured as a friend
and as a lover to behave.

CONSCIENCE

The wood holds dangers
darker than the dentist's chair
love is still the eye
of anything worthwhile
                    or worth having
and so we keep that one eye open.

And knowing that it goes by
multitudes of attitudes and names
it's wise to learn and not forget
the favorite name for love is conscience.

Conscience being the first thing
Christ conceived for us
must mean *love* is Christmas
by another name.

WOMEN IN WINTER

The winter has widened
and it won't be easy.
Nearly everywhere the city's closing up.
Old women come down to the park
their hands withered, gnarled, broken
scarves and handkerchiefs wrapped
                round and round them
offer no protection.

But they have to rise each day
from their empty lifeless beds
and shuffle through the streets
if only just to prove the hours
left to them
are hours they can hold.

They are
not friendless
certain people
of a certain kind
observe their comings
and their goings
block to block
until they
        come no more.

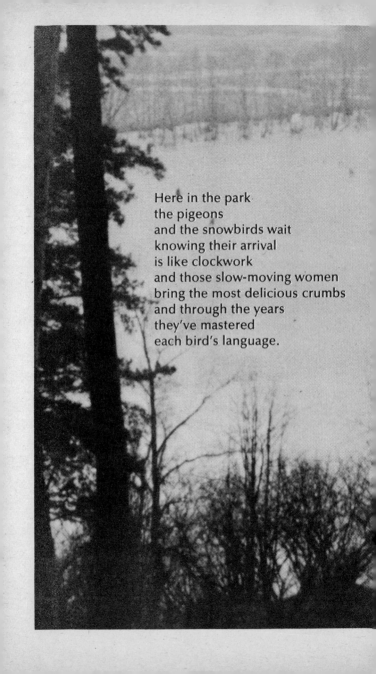

Here in the park
the pigeons
and the snowbirds wait
knowing their arrival
is like clockwork
and those slow-moving women
bring the most delicious crumbs
and through the years
they've mastered
each bird's language.

Somewhere in the bags
these women carry firmly
there is a crumb or cracker
set aside for each bird waiting.

Even in the snow
and ice bound streets
when no one else
dares venture out
the women don't forget
their friends
the now-much-less-in-number
                          birds.

To be a snowbound bird
confined within this city
would not be bad at all,
does not always mean
the welfare roles, the dole.
For there are always
              certain women
old in years,
but young in friendship
who carry festive
              shopping bags
containing mysteries and magic
and every kind of tasty crumb
who never miss
appointed rounds.

The Sea, as an Observer

for ANITA KERR

If friendship is but the shadow of the
evening—as I believe it is—think how deep
the night becomes—and deeper with the
years. I caution you to start providing for the
late years in your life by concerning yourself
with finding early one or two people you can
count on, nurturing them, then growing with
them year on year, providing for them as
surely they'll provide for you. Some you'll lose
to argument and age. Others die or grow their
own way. That way may be away from you . . .
I cannot tell you how to stop them going.

NEGATIVE

I have carried several oceans
in my head for company
so that when I found myself
within the middle earth
I'd have water,
wide and deep enough
to wash the dirt
from every chamber
of my brain.

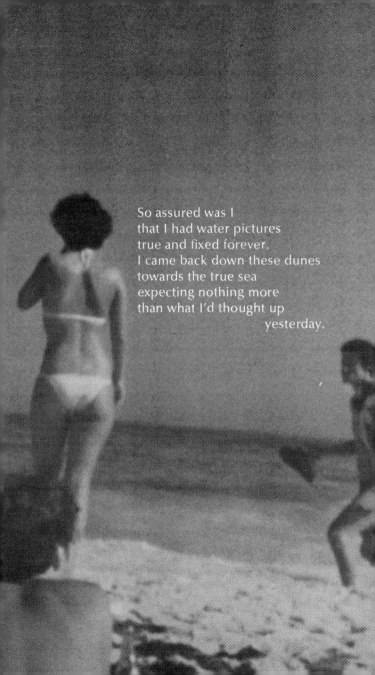

So assured was I
that I had water pictures
true and fixed forever.
I came back down these dunes
towards the true sea
expecting nothing more
than what I'd thought up
                              yesterday.

But no one knows the ocean
unless they're sinking into it.
The shore is only shore
if you walk from it
to the ocean's edge and past
to be covered by its real
and not imagined wetness.
And so I cannot trust
my surest memory of you.

What did we have,
love at first
        and then some habit
and in-between purgatory need?
What made us come together?
        Can you say for sure?

Stay within the darkness
                and from me
just a while longer
and you'll be
only one more pond
I thought to be an ocean.
Come to me
and our collective ocean
will wash across our days
                and troubles.

I'm not sure
I believe that
but it's hard to let
so much lived
        and unlived life
go without a speech.

A pity all things started
cannot finish at the summit.
Our lack of understanding
        one the other
leaves us by the roadside
as the giant wave goes by.

The holidays
are now beginning,
decorations everywhere.
What better time
to just let go?

I'll miss our language
and the lack of it
but I would rather
walk the empty
midnight street
than share your
Christmas frown,
or sail the charted seas
Santa at my elbow—
the Christ child fixed
Forever in my mind.

Missing you
I did not miss Christmas
a lifetime, maybe
but not one single birthday
of the Christ child.

They say
a comet's coming
through the sky
before the Twelfth Night
                    passes.
We needn't stay here
waiting for a signal
            or a sign.
What is finished
should be finally finished
not hung onto like a lifeline
that has finally stretched
            and snapped.

BEACH DIARY, 1

The sun full measured
this second day
of this fourth year
of coming back
    and coming back
and coming back again
        to Mexico.

In the trees it crouches now
        until it springs out
harsher than remembered
to bake me through the noon.

Siestas notwithstanding
the heat has got them all
impatient, amorous
                    or ambitious.

Lizards in the patio
squaring off at either end
then racing down the tile
towards each other,
hind ends reared
and hind legs stiffened,
they snap and scatter
in the dance of courtship.

In the end
like movie dinosaurs
they clash and roll
in twisted knots
the balance of the afternoon.

Having seen the ritual
acted out and realized
I started back to sleep
beneath the kindest sky
I've known in twenty months.

Suddenly they're in the hedge.
Rustling, threading through
                    the roots.
Tunneling
in the dead-leaf carpeting.
                    Whoosh,
and one comes flying
through the thicket
like an alligator given wings.

At midday
a school of dolphins
surface sink and zigzag by
heading northward in the noon
then back again at sunset.

Too far out to swim to
but close enough to see
arching up and down
                amid the waves
like tumblers in a circus,
who hit the net
then bounce into the air
                and somersault again.

Later
when the sun
starts slumping seaward
it will be the gulls' turn
to file through the air
in bad formation.

Not as agile as the sparrows
nor as graceful as wild geese
jetting home at spring,
these troop transport gulls
                        are clumsy.

Fuel tanks full
you can almost see
their sleep beginning
as they fly, no, stumble by.

Sand crabs again
          scrambling sideways
dragging battered burdens
through the soft red sunset.
A fish head gorged up by a gull
twice the sand crab's size.
Another darts off easily
with half a clam.

My long shadow
passing past them
is enough to send each recluse
down his well-dug hole.

Could I invade this spider diary
I might turn up
the seashore chronicle
of one whole winter
or a pattern more elaborate
than the tank-like tracks
of a thousand sand crabs
invading that first atoll
past and all along
                the shoreline.

Evening
and a single gecko's
loud percussion
heard above the waves
       above the wind
above the crickets,
not yet chorusing
but making ready.

Geckos everywhere.
Between the roof beams
along the stuccoed wall
above the arch
of every doorway.

A dozen now. More.
Pale off-white in color
            almost yellow.
Only slightly darker
than the once-white plaster.

Hanging on,
upside down and sideways.
Not moving, not sleeping.
Geckos. Not like crystal.
Not hard like alabaster.
More like marzipan.
Fragile-looking.

The gecko's
vocal clattering
somewhere beyond
            the shutters
never seems
to get an answer.
            He clicks
at all the unexpected times
like castanets gone crazy
and without a master.

He's been here since
                the pinto morning.
Little runs he makes
then stopping to survey
a bee or fly
his long tongue
takes them by surprise
quicker and more sure
than any angler.
                Agile as an angel.

The gecko sounds again.
The echo through the arches
                    could be one or five.
Tambourines in double time.

I half expect
that Spanish dancers
will come bursting through the door,
vests and petticoats of every color
heels stomping, snapping, clicking
ready for some fine fiesta.

The day
has opened up,
progressed and gone.
I've watched it move
from the lizard's lost siesta
to Don Quixote of La Mancha's
imagined but not-held
                    fiesta.

Stars.
A few are falling.
No comet yet,
but it's expected.

BEACH DIARY, 2

With the stars
all stringing out and strung
and the moon half hung
                    and hanging,
hunger starts somewhere
within my belly.
It will not be gone
with bowls of guacamole,
            as it didn't go
with friends and family
commiserating on my loss.

I elected
to come down
to this house
and to this beach
knowing that I couldn't
leave all memory,
            fact or fiction
in an overcoat at home.

Soon the crickets
will stop adding,
counting, summing up.

The heavy air will set all things
          to sleeping
and the steady rhythm
of this well-loved,
          well-known ocean
will conspire to keep us there.

That battle won,
another day makes ready
          to arrive,
another night to follow.

More defeats
or maybe victories
        wait ahead.
I will have to meet
and battle each alone,
but the victory party
isn't worth the having
if the celebration's done
        in solitary.

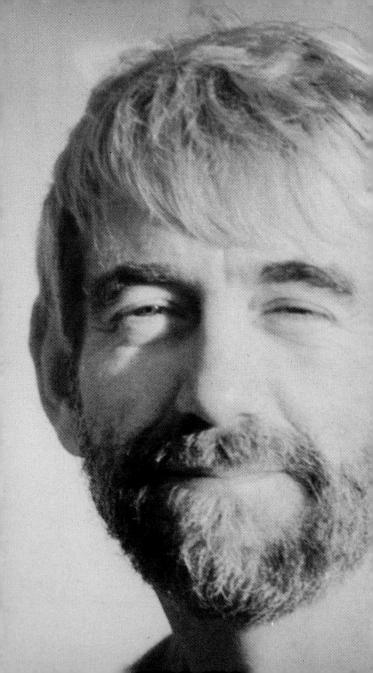

BEACH DIARY, 3

Was there rehearsal,
a time of trying out
how many starts
and stops occurred
before the balls
fell into place
and boisterous
        breakwater
turned to gentle surf?

Awhile back.
But how far back
        and when?
These questions done
and finally answered
I hope they'll not
be asked again.

Words once written
        on a page
and published
cannot be taken back—
        or altered
though each of us
invents a way
to prove we're moving
ahead if not beyond.

Strangers
catch us running
then bring us
to a stop,
demanding to know
what a certain sentence
or a long line meant.
They speak aloud
a favorite poem
heard or read and then
remembered to the line break.
And that feels good
        or doesn't
depending on the friend
                you're with
and trying to impress.

Like
the dirty foam
that caps the whitecaps
collecting grime
and all the smaller
things that float,
critics have their place
but only if they
              set about
redefining and reviewing
not your life
            or life-style
but what they call
              your work,
otherwise
critics should be
                sneezed at
especially if you have
                  a cold.

The best of them
        are guardians
            not guards.
The difference
is a subtle one.
A guardian protects,
advises and reports.
A guard is posted
to keep out
or not let in.

Always listen and evaluate
the guardian's instructions.
Beware and be wary
        of the guards.
Not even dogs
who walk beside them
are approachable and friendly.

Scaling Walls

for SKIP REDWINE

Friendship consists of *being* a friend, not having a friend. And so it is that friendship means loving rather than being loved. The gifts that one receives for giving are so immeasurable that it is almost an injustice to accept them.

VACANT LOT

Coming through
the twice-cracked concrete
in the vacant lot next door,
a sprig, not quite a tree
but strong and growing stronger
surviving where a house
                could not survive.
The house was trucked away
                    last summer
board by board and brick by brick.

I never knew the family living there
as I've not had communion
with most communes
congregated on this street.
Anyway, a sprig—
                 not quite a tree
is more sociable than any family
save a family of grass.
Not as friendly
as a well-loved animal,
but equal to the task
of being loved and loving.

OFTEN IN WINTER

Often in winter
that feared but unseen hand
old banker priests can still depend on
to help them herd their flocks
up the steps of stained-glass banks,
returns dependably
to work me over too.

Christ knows my span of concentration
and the time to teach me lessons
is the time when I'm boxed in by grey.
For when the sun shines
what man fears God
or his one begotten Son?

Loving is the new salvation,
with Gideon the king providing Bibles
for each final prayer and evensong.
And bedroom soldiers
on ten million battlefields
fighting nightly sword to sword
would not dispute
their uncrowned monarch.

I presume
that International Harvester
can take its proper credit
for bales of straw and wheat.

But man must not forget
who fostered love
        and fed it.
He did.

POINT OF REFERENCE

What frame of reference
do we now assign to time?
A traveling plane,
a space in which to travel,
a counter for counterpoints,
an instrument for saving age.
A means of remembering
a tunnel to forget,
proof of our existence
further proof that we
do not exist
and will stop existing.

Time is nothing without clocks.
Break the wristwatch
and the aging still continues,
but time grows muddled
                and confused.
Pull the blind on sunshine
and the dark will keep us
in the middle night.
Without a calendar
we have only cold to show us
when the first full winter day
                arrives.

The engine coughs, wheezes, stops,
the heart within the body
            shrinks or slows
then finally halts,
the traffic light still works
or fails on unseen meters
based on timing and on time.

And time is nothing
            without clocks.

Suitcases in Hallways

for LAURA EASTMAN

We may not meet again within the coming year. Now is the time for us to take advantage of our started friendship—in all the best ways we know how and can learn about together.

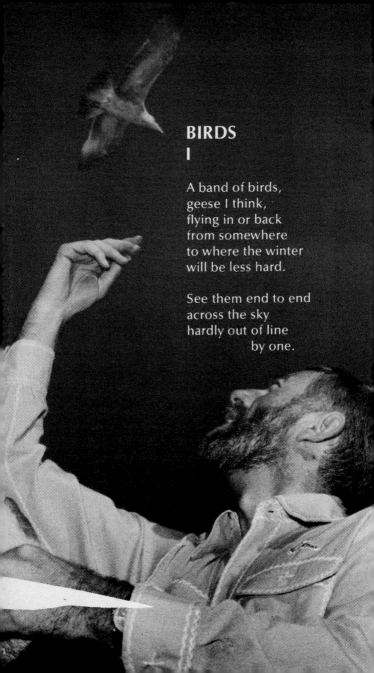

BIRDS
I

A band of birds,
geese I think,
flying in or back
from somewhere
to where the winter
will be less hard.

See them end to end
across the sky
hardly out of line
      by one.

Like a victory sign but wider
their formation is a marvel,
meticulous, mechanical.

And there
just above those trees
another band of birds
brings up the rear,
like a vanguard
keeping guard.

Some have landed,
and they rest
on bare-limbed trees
and telephone lines.
They dot but never blur
                    the moon.

Perched still and silent
awaiting their rotation,
strung out they spy
            in Morse code.

II

Rested, restless now
they move as one.
Picking up formation
they fly straight forward
                overhead
blinking in the sunlight
till a better place to perch
                is found.

I stumbled on your suitcase
            in the hallway
half an hour ago.
Have you been looking
out the window
            at the birds?

I have seen you move so often.
Set sail on so much
                unknown sea
that I can feel the readiness
within you to be gone
but this time
I'll do all the running.
You needn't fly or migrate
                with the birds.

Stay.
I wish you life
in great abundance
down your lifetime.
Whoever's coming,
known or unknown
on his way to you
I pray that he
will not be long
in finding you.

Don't forget
to send a postcard
telling me the news.
Did the seals
come back this year,
did the grunion run
and did you out-distance
all the near and distant strangers,
capture them and captivate them
                    one by one?

Write me.
I'd be unhappy if I thought
that you were still out running
and had not been caught.

Tomorrow
I'll be that lone bird
winging past the morning moon
on my way below
the belt of California.

EARTH

Alive, awake
we anguish for the dead
we wail and weep.
But it is for ourselves
                    that tears
and tearing at the heart
                        is done.

We do not grieve
because the earth
reclaims its own.
We weep because
we're suddenly deprived
of good companions
        sound judgment
and familiar counsel.

TWENTY-SEVEN

The fireflies gone now
the trees low bending
with the weight
of winter rain
I listen for the sound
of winters past.
The years I walked
the rainy streets
and filtered through
           the parks
in search of music people.
Creeping home to bed alone
to be with imaginary lovers
and hear the sound of Eden
ringing in my young ears.

I could go back to San Francisco
if I still had muscled thighs.
The trouble is
        I run a little faster now.

Some
Come as Friends...But

Friendship shouldn't come too easy—or if it
does, *go easy* slower even than the
photograph coming from the negative.

OURSELVES TO KNOW

Our losses are the sores
we box and bottle up
far back, ladder down
amid the unlit chambers
of our cluttered minds,
hoping they'll stay lost
                    or unrecovered
like the mother lode
of some as yet uncovered
                    mine.

Those things first dear to us
              then lost
no matter what the reason
go unlisted in our wills
            and codicils.

No pirates bearing half a map
find the other half marked *x*.
The interview is over
when the questions
            come too close.
Grudges come
and settle in with ease
when losses are the subject.

We wear our gains
           like barfly gear
or rows of medals
on an unpatched shirt.

Hurt, like loss,
is no brother
to ill attention,
the more we leave it
unrepaired and unattended
the quicker it will go.

It leaves behind
at most a residue
like sediment
           that bubbles
at the bottom of the wine.

Why is it then
that simple sorrows
seem to thrive
as though the weekend gardener
          was charged
with keeping them alive.

One snub
and every act of joy
once raised in toast
and sweetly celebrated
is crushed into the never was.

Friends are not immune
to this ill treatment
and lovers bear the brunt.
Acquaintances
remain immune to arson
even as the ashes smolder.
Not yet close enough
for love or final friendship,
they remain unblemished
                and unblamed.

Why make tedium
safer than it should be,
constant, crossfiled,
                calibrated
dried and dreary
hauled out in a hurry
dusted off and fluffed
like paper flowers
that go unnoticed
as counterfeit and crude
until the posy paper
                    tears
or the paint upon the plastic
wears thin and peels
enough to warrant touching up.

Reality is square
and easy to make out.
Its shadings are
the works of men
imbibed with building
barricades and battlements.

The more we hide
our summits or our sorrows
the less of what we are
                    or can be
is reflected or looks back at us
                          from mirrors.

Pause
before you give up seeking
the exit to the maze
send the guard or guide dog
off to chase a bone.

Be unafraid to leave
some portions of your life
to fate, to change, to God.
Should a friend's behavior
                    worry you
you may at last be given
the chance to give
some friendship back.

Some unexpected love
arriving right on time
is more welcome to the ill
                    than penicillin.

We know ourselves
but we'd know our worth
and, yes, our worthlessness
better if we paused
with more regularity
to take the boards from off
the shuttered windows
and let some sunlight in.

The worth of man
is not in how he treats himself
or his dearest dozen friends
but how, when it is offered him,
he treats the treat of giving.

SOME THOUGHTS ON FINDING MY CAR BROKEN INTO ONE SUNDAY MORNING AROUND THE CORNER FROM THE HUNGRY i

How well I sang my songs that night
the audience was quiet to a man
I felt some kinship with all people
until I went into the dark
and found that like Enrico says
it is a jungle after all
and there are animals of prey
we've not yet named.

Whoever slit the belly
of that wild young mustang
and hoped to find a treasure
got instead a meager haul.

They took the things I value most
my toothbrush and a razor
some poems and a song
I'd stuffed up in a suitcase
together with a list of names
I'd been ten years collecting—
no good to anyone but me.

What a fire it will make
that antique address book
those names that have no faces
and now I'll judge my popularity
by those who ring *me* up.

What pawn shop of the mind
can index all those names and numbers
gathered in a month,
a week, a lifetime?
New People in the last four days
are all the ones that I remember.

Enrico says the worst thing is
that some dark stranger
pored among my things
and has a knowledge of
my secret self.

Insurance covers underwear
suits and shaving kits
the latest Catherine Sauvage disc
but who's to put a premium
on notebooks full of foolish things
a pasted joke an anecdote
a lyric started not yet sung.

That address book thick and black
I'd like to have it back
for it contains old and worn
a laundry list of love.

ON BORROWING

A man is killed in Hindustan
I feel the bullet in my head.
A child is crying in the street
her tears could be my own.
I know that animals help man
when slaughtered
            on the doctor's couch
but dead dogs by the roadside
stay with me for days.

I find it hard to understand
why someone takes my words
        from me.
            A friend?
Once upon a time he was
but then he stole my sea
                and my zodiacs as well.
                        Ideas are few
another might not come by soon.

I had a pet raccoon
who took
my toothbrush once
but only
to another room.

IDLE UNDER SUN

Once I thought
ideas were exceptions
      not the rule.
That is not so.
Ideas are so plentiful
that they ride by
      on air.
You've only to reach out
and snatch one
from the mist
or from nowhere.

With little raw material
                    but sand
the sea has made
two hundred thousand
                    mountains
that we'll likely never know.

This being so
is it too much to ask
that each man in his lifetime
make a single contribution,
both unique and useful,
that no man
walking down the beach
has handed us before?

Why not pay back
　　　　our birth bill
by adding an idea
　　　　even two or six
to the many given us
without condition
　　　　or a price?

⚓ ⚓ ⚓

Lifted Aloft

for ANN BARZEL

Carrying a friend upon your back you are
carried, lifted aloft yourself.

BY THE NUMBERS

You went away
in such great numbers.

A covey of you
at the corner.
A band of you
beyond the block.
A herd of you
unhearing as I cried aloud,
come back, come back.

You went away so often
and in such great numbers
that I'd not be surprised
to meet a regiment of you
clicking down the sidewalk
clacking up the street
returning, coming back.

TORCHLIGHT

Chaos calls for celebration
as order calls for quiet.
Seldom when the nation's
                    troubled
will the masses riot.

On occasion
when bright bonfires
light the night for hoboes' warmth
and heroes in the forest
celebrating with a victory supper
the peasant, uninformed,
will draw his own conclusions
deciding that the skirmish
            on the far-off hill
belongs to that long-delayed
revolution revolving in his head.

The railroad war
          is over,
civilians have returned
          to civility,
the barricades
are down or falling.
Guns are not imported now
but exported from
          great factories
made by aid from
every country
wanting peace.

What a pity
we can't tell
the revolutionary
that the war was lost
    without him.

What a pity
we can't say
and be believed
that we live
not in peace
but between two wars.
The last one barely done
the next one coming,
stumbling down the country
            or the block
        but on its way.

War arrives
it can be expected,
it's a-borning
if not tomorrow
then the morning after.
Why is it
that we need to see
the near fields
and those farther off
ablaze amid mid-August
                    sun
before we realize
the battle has begun.

And will we ever know
how many wars
man has made mistakenly
                  or anyway
three weeks early.

I myself
while waiting for a call
        that never came
have thought as minutes
turned to dreaded days
that had I killed
        the telephone,
there would have been
no reason for
the smallest seed of hate
to work its way through or into
a brain cell I'd reserved
                    for love.

AUGUST 7

There will be revolutions
we can touch one day
instead of only those
that timidly touch us.

Revolutions made in fold-down beds
that slide into the closet
                    from the guilty day.
Rallies done for freedom
    from the fear of those
        who try their best
            to push us from
                each other.

Then I'll vote Republican
and you'll be older too
and both of us will try
to walk our children
through the world
we've just come through.

They'll protest as we have done
that their lives are theirs.
And they'll be just as right
                          as we are now.

But every generation gap
should have some kind of bridge
even if it's only made of love.

ENTR'ACTE

We were in love that summer
and birds about the sky
were singing with themselves,
carols I cannot remember,
though I do recall
the color of the trees
and the things I thought
but never said to you.

I thought of San Francisco
and the bridge being painted
even when it wasn't Spring.
I thought about
the loneliness of oceans,
of Colorado snow
and writing a book called
                    Where Can I Go.
Everything but us.
We were a fact
and not to be embellished on,
or thought about.

Now I remember
you liked brandy
and Bruckner
          and beer,
and painting Mt. Baker
as it sank into the fog.

You liked little boys
and skipping breakfast
unless we made it
for ourselves.

In that whole season
as warm day followed warm day
I never thought about
tomorrow or next year.
Of course you never do
when it's happening for you,
and it was happening
for both of us.

When did we stumble,
where did we turn
when did we stop
as though we hadn't yet begun?

It was, I think,
somewhere near
September's end.
Other people started
getting in between us,
almost as though
we hadn't locked the gate.

Thinking back now
I may have even come upon
an answer to the *why*.
Sometimes being happy
seems a self-indulgence.
When on every side of you
the world seems wrapped
                    in wrong,
it becomes a bending burden
to go on smiling
or to smile at all
even for the one you love;
but we ought to try.

We had friends
who never laughed,
not because there was a war—
                               there was,
but then there always is.

Friends who found
excuses for us
as to why we shouldn't be
laughing and together.
Friends who'd fire
the final bullet
into each of us
if they were asked.

It was something
very simple really,
fun had lost
a button off its pants,
not the first one,
and none of us
was making any effort
to sew it on again.

Night Mischief

for GEORGIA SHELDON

Friendship never wears a mask. It removes the necessity for masquerading and false faces.

NIGHT MISCHIEF

A young man
standing in the rain
outside that so familiar
                    window
known to me
because I've lived
across the street from it
too many years, too long.

Known to me
because it's unlike
any other window,
and what stays or sits
or struts behind/beyond it
is familiar if not known to me.

My domain
is not my own
not because it isn't shared
although it isn't
but because it isn't shared
by her.

I should have moved
the day I saw her
gliding up the stairs alone
or later every time I saw
someone come or go
beneath her balcony,
down those stairs,
or coming round the corner
on the sidewalk or the street
overtipping taxi drivers
as they found the right house
and dropped their passengers
four feet from the door.

Good woman
you do me damage.
Angels could not force
such sense of loss upon me
whatever their conspiracy.

Just now
the door is answered
and the young man
          steps inside.
Outside
the rain still falls
and not uncomfortably.

Long ago
I should have moved away
or else I should have
walked across the street
                    myself
smiled and told her
how she was an interruption
                    in my life
because she lived there
just the other side of it.

Without the chance
for real rejection
          she rejected me.
Without a *no*
she let me know.

BROWN OCTOBER

Leaves fall down now
brown and beautiful
brittle to the touch
lying on the ground
of filling public fountains.
Swirling down the street,
catching in the gutters
and diverting little streams
of water.

Brown October leaves
trampled under foot
banged about by brooms
that sweep the gutters clean.

I remembered today
that among the silly things
                    you saved
was a brown and yellow leaf
pressed between
the pages of a book somewhere.

We found it in the park,
                    remember?

I shook out every book I owned
to find it. Still it's lost,
or owned these days
by Hemingway or Whitman.
Maybe even Gertrude Stein.
Would she know what to do
with a brown and yellow leaf?
And would she give it back?

SEVEN ON A SUMMER BEACH

Wes the learner made mistakes
but with his youth to cushion him
he always fell to safety.

Murphy's plumber tools were shiny.
Every other week he went,
coming back on even weeks
to tell us how his time was spent.

Bill believed in nothing
except the pots and bowls and busts
that he could conjure out of clay
with his own hands.

223

Others in our circle.
Newt who tried to be a poet
and with his dying
              finally was.
Buck with all the morals
                 of a rabbit.
In his head a haunted house
locked with secret secrets
                  to this day.

Lenny lived
above the boardwalk
and cooked all day
lending me his room
              two blocks away,
teaching me while he was there,
leaving me to learn alone
when he was gone.

Seven on a summer beach
that stretched the length
           of Santa Monica.
Sunday to Sunday we lived
seventeen summers ago.

Even then my songs were starting
to be only those
of my invention,
made for me
and my small audience
           of friends.

The next song coming
I would always breathe up
from the bottom of my belly
        with all the air I had.

Out of the army, out of work,
I was trained for nothing,
not even the saying of words
or the singing of songs.
But dreams are cheap enough to come by
and I had storefronts full of those.

Dream I did
along that Sunday beach
and then sun-saturated
joined the others in the bar.
My unemployment checks now gone
Bill always bought the beer
I nursed the first two hours
till some new friend
would buy another.

Then years later
              each time we met
he still reminded me
that in my early life
he'd been St. Benefactor
                    of the Beer.

Of the seven
Bill was first to marry.
None of us expected it
but all of us were pleased
                    and proud.
By then the two of us
had passed from being friends.
After all, I'd sponged
and in his mind was wanting.
What I wondered then.
What I wonder now.

I hope that in Bill's union
there are no guilty parties.

Lenny goes on cooking
                    for all I know.
Probably the chef supreme
with apprentices of every kind.

I hope he's teaching them
all the lessons he taught me,
truths so valuable and ingrained
I'd be hard pressed to call them up
or list them one on one by name.

He called once when I was gone.

There are those who've told
                    and tell me
I've been gone some time.

Murphy went on drinking
till half a glass at evening
became a bottle, finally two.
And evening started on awakening
and ended when he went to sleep.
Not long ago he drifted back,
came into town and stayed a time,
then like his rusty plumber's tools
                              was gone.
I think the only one he saw was Wes.

Even now the horror
of Murphy's gentle giant head
shot through with shot-glass webbing
is hard for me to understand.
I'll never know his like again
        if I even knew it then.

Buck went back to Indiana.
He wrote me once to say
the hunting wasn't great but good
and shouldn't I come there
and shouldn't I give up the city
and be another country Robin Hood?

One year Newt sent out
            a Christmas card
that showed him
taking one long walk
along our old familiar beach.
Printed on it
was a paragraph that said
here there is a tree
I want some unborn child to see.

Some years later he was dead,
cut down by person or persons
yet unknown to anyone but him.

I grieve for him
because I always promised
                    him and me
that if I made it
I'd find an audience somewhere
for all the things I knew he'd write.
He left no will and all his poetry
is still locked in the ground
                    inside his head.
Sure wasn't much of a funeral,
even the flowers were dying.
                    He said that too.
And I remember further
that all he asked from any friend
was a patchwork quilt of hope.

Wes and I are left.
          Two from seven.
Our lives could not be
more different/more alike.
Passing forty in the same
               two-month span,
we've both grown beards.
We both have semisteady hands.
Each of us is bored with beaching
and the wasted time it takes
               to cultivate a tan.
I like him better now
we have a kinship,
having both survived.

Married life
wears well on him,
he's fatter and he laughs
and finally he's that little boy
he used to such perfection
back when he was just another one of us
shaking sand from out his socks
and following friendly enemies
everywhere and home.

If I smile too much
my friend corrects my grin
but I love Wes enough now
to find no single thing in him
                    to censure.

That leaves me.

I am where I left off
a month, an hour ago.
My lament is yet unwritten
                    therefore still not sung.
It does not come up from my stomach
                                easily.
Could I put it into one long line
I'd have to say that what I longed for
                    knowing it or not
is out there somewhere out of reach
and day by day, week by week,
I lose the Jason urge to start the chase.

It may be
the one I have imagined
          or imagine not
will, on some quiet afternoon
                    or silent night
when this old house resounds
or fails to echo with the small noise
          I make on my own,
finding this place, know enough
to come in slowly, unafraid
and share with me a certain kind
                    of silence.

GOOD EVENING, FRIEND

How good it feels
to concentrate
on others.

Foreigners or farmers
women in the street
and those within my head.
Lumberjacks and loudmouths.
Mothers chasing children
and the child working
at eluding parents, making mischief
of the mischief being made
on them.

Lovers courting
squaring off
within the dance
then dancing circles
round each other.
Pairing off
then repairing
to their corners,
exchanging partners
in the dance
or tripping through the day
not as dancers
but as audience
to those who love
and live their life loves
out before the world.

What a time
this end of summertime
to just observe
to call the world my friend
and let imaginary friendships
          tumble in my head.

Friendships needn't be that real
except within our minds.
A friend can be a fig tree
and never know it,
a special place
within a certain wood
a special tree
within that selfsame forest.

A friendship
is a seed once sown
that's better cultivated
in the practice.

How many Augusts
I have taken to my heart
            as friends
would more than fill
a calendar completely made
            of Augusts.

How many people
walking in as many
            different leas
I've learned to call
sweet friend and gentle foe
will go unmarked
not jotted down
for they have happened
in that gold brown month
so often that no diary
            or Polaroid
could hold them or catch them
            in four minutes.

Computers not yet made
and ancient abacuses
will not print out
or count for me
their numbers and their names.

I have a singular
satisfaction in knowing
there are friends I've made
and lost and made again
without their knowledge.

Good evening, friend.
Ah ha, you didn't catch me
or discern that bond
                    between us
or did you?

About the Author

ROD McKUEN'S books of poetry have sold in excess of 20,000,000 copies in hardcover, making him the best-selling and most widely read poet of our times. In addition, his poetry is taught and studied in schools, colleges, universities, and seminaries throughout the world.

Mr. McKuen is the composer of nearly 2,000 songs which have been widely translated. They include: "Jean," "Love's Been Good to Me," "The Importance of the Rose," "Rock Gently," "Ally, Ally, Oxen Free," and several dozen songs written with the late French composer Jacques Brel, including "If You Go Away," "Come Jef," "Port of Amsterdam," and "Seasons in the Sun." Both writers have termed their writing habits together as three distinct methods: collaboration, adaptation, and translation.

Mr. McKuen's film music has twice been nominated for Motion Picture Academy Awards ("The Prime of Miss Jean Brodie" and "A Boy Named Charlie Brown") and his classical work—including symphonies, concertos, piano sonatas, and his popular *Adagio for Harp and Strings*—is performed by leading orchestras. In May, 1972, the London Royal Philharmonic premiered his *Concerto No. 3 for Piano and Orchestra* and a suite, *The Plains of My Country*. In 1973 the Louisville Orchestra commissioned Mr. McKuen to compose a suite for orchestra and narrator entitled *The City;* it was subsequently nominated for a Pulitzer Prize.

His *Symphony No. 3*, commissioned by the Menninger Foundation in honor of its fiftieth anniversary, was premiered in 1975 in Topeka, Kansas.

The author has completed the libretto and music for a full-length musical, "The Black Eagle."

In July, 1976, two new McKuen works were premiered at St. Giles Church, Cripplegate, in the city of London: a *Concerto for Cello and Orchestra;* and the first major symphonic composition written for synthesizer and symphony orchestra, *Concerto for Balloon and Orchestra.*

In 1978 Mr. McKuen was named by the University of Detroit for his humanitarian work and in Washington was presented The Carl Sandburg Award by the National Platform Association as "the outstanding people's poet, because he has made poetry a part of so many people's lives in this country."

In 1978 and 1979 Mr. McKuen spent nearly a year in the Soviet Union working on the musical score for twenty hours of television entitled "The Unknown War." He was also the co-adapter with producer Fred Weiner of the series' scripts.

In addition to this book, the author has completed this year a new volume about America entitled *The Power Bright and Shining* and a work he terms, a declaration of faith, *An Outstretched Hand.*

As a concert artist he toured Great Britain, France and Australia and covered both political conventions. Two new ballets by Mr. McKuen were presented by The American Dance Ensemble in Pittsburgh, and in Brussels their opera company began to gear up for the premier of his opera *A Black Eagle* to be presented in both English and French.

Finally, the author-composer has nearly completed his new collection of poetry entitled *Too Many Midnights* which will be an original paperback from Pocket Books.

SOURCES

Index to First Lines

We appreciate your continued acceptance of the works of

Rod McKuen

As a way of saying "THANKS" we'd like to send you a complimentary *free* full-length album—no strings attached . . . only a $2.00 charge for postage and handling. We think it's something you'll especially like . . .

- - - - - - - - - - - - - - - - - - - -

Maybe you think you own all of Rod McKuen's work . . . but some of the books are only available through mail order.

Beyond The Boardwalk

Hardcover $6.95 ☐
Quality paperback $3.95 ☐

Moment To Moment

Quality paperback $3.95 ☐

And Autumn Came

This special edition originally published at $50.00. *Rod's first book of poetry* in unusual delux gift set—hard bound, hand lettered, beautifully illustrated. Each copy signed and numbered, boxed and stamped in 24 karat gold, 12 x 12. Now only $19.95. A beautiful gift for yourself or someone you love.

Special limited edition $19.95 ☐